HOW TO DO SUBSTITUTE TEACHING IN CHICAGO

By

Helen Marie Prahl

ISBN: 1-4033-4496-5 (e-book)
ISBN: 1-4033-4497-3 (Paperback)
ISBN: 1-4033-4498-1 (Hardcover)

This book is printed on acid free paper.

1stBooks – rev. 10/20/03